DRAWING DINOSAURS

DRAWING T. REX

AND OTHER MEAT-EATING DINOSAURS

STEVE BEAUMONT

PowerKiDS
press

New York

Published in 2010 by The Rosen Publishing Group, Inc.
29 East 21st Street, New York, NY 10010

Copyright © 2010 Arcturus Publishing Ltd

Artwork and text: Steve Beaumont
Editor (Arcturus): Carron Brown
Designer: Steve Flight

Library of Congress Cataloging-in-Publication Data

Beaumont, Steve.
  Drawing T. rex and other meat-eating dinosaurs / Steve Beaumont. —
1st ed.
      p. cm. — (Drawing dinosaurs)
  Includes index.
  ISBN 978-1-61531-907-7 (library binding) — ISBN 978-1-4488-0434-4 (pbk.) —
ISBN 978-1-4488-0435-1 (6-pack)
  1. Dinosaurs in art—Juvenile literature. 2. Drawing—Technique—Juvenile literature.
  3. Tyrannosaurus rex—Juvenile literature. I. Title.
  NC780.5.B394 2010
  743.6—dc22
                                        2009033264

Printed in China

CPSIA compliance information: Batch #AW0102PK : For further information contact Rosen Publishing, New York, New York at 1-800-237-9932

CONTENTS

"**D**inosaurs"… the word conjures up all kinds of powerful and exciting images. From the terrifying jaws of *Tyrannosaurus rex* to the sharp beak of Oviraptor and the fast-running, sharp-clawed Velociraptor—dinosaurs came in all shapes and sizes.

These amazing creatures ruled Earth for over 160 million years until, suddenly, they all died out. No one has ever seen a living, moving, roaring dinosaur, but thanks to the research of paleontologists, who piece together dinosaur fossils, we now have a pretty good idea what many of them looked like.

Some were as big as huge buildings, others had enormous teeth, scaly skin, horns, claws, and body armor. Dinosaurs have played starring roles in books, on television, and in blockbuster movies, and now it's time for them to take center stage on your drawing pad!

In this book we've chosen three incredible meat-eating dinosaurs for you to learn how to draw. We've also included a dinosaur landscape for you to sketch, so you can really set the prehistoric scene for your drawings.

You'll find advice on the essential drawing tools you'll need to get started, tips on how to get the best results from your drawings, and easy-to-follow step-by-step instructions showing you how to draw each dinosaur. So, it's time to bring these extinct monsters back to life—let's draw some dinosaurs!

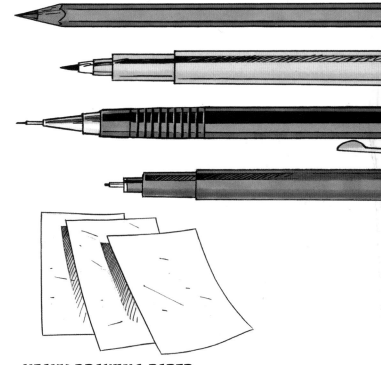

DRAWING TOOLS

Let's start with the essential drawing tools you'll need to create awesome illustrations. Build up your collection as your drawing skills improve.

LAYOUT PAPER

Artists, both as professionals and as students, rarely produce their first practice sketches on their best quality art paper. It's a good idea to buy some inexpensive plain letter-size paper from a stationery store for all of your practice sketches. Buy the least expensive kind.

Most professional illustrators use cheaper paper for basic layouts and practice sketches before they get to the more serious task of producing a masterpiece on more costly material.

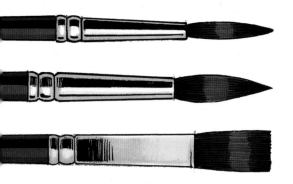

HEAVY DRAWING PAPER

This paper is ideal for your final version. You don't have to buy the most expensive brand—most decent arts and crafts stores will stock their own brand or another lower-priced brand and unless you're thinking of turning professional, these will work fine.

WATERCOLOR PAPER

This paper is made from 100 percent cotton and is much higher quality than wood-based papers. Most arts and crafts stores will stock a large range of weights and sizes—140 pounds per ream (300 g/sq m) will be fine.

LINE ART PAPER

If you want to practice black and white ink drawing, line art paper enables you to produce a nice clear crisp line. You'll get better results than you would on heavier paper as it has a much smoother surface.

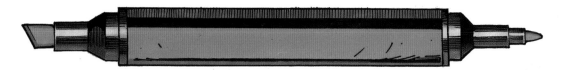

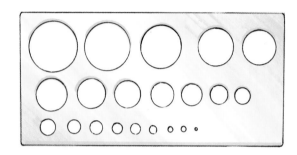

PENCILS

It's best not to cut corners on quality here. Get a good range of graphite (lead) pencils ranging from soft (#1) to hard (#4).

Hard lead lasts longer and leaves less graphite on the paper. Soft lead leaves more lead on the paper and wears down more quickly. Every artist has his personal preference, but #2.5 pencils are a good medium grade to start out with until you find your own favorite.

Spend some time drawing with each grade of pencil and get used to their different qualities. Another good product to try is the clutch, or mechanical pencil. These are available in a range of lead thicknesses, 0.5mm being a good medium size. These pencils are very good for fine detail work.

PENS

There is a large range of good quality pens on the market and all will do a decent job of inking. It's important to experiment with a range of different pens to determine which you find most comfortable to work with.

You may find that you end up using a combination of pens to produce your finished piece of artwork. Remember to use a pen that has waterproof ink if you want to color your illustration with a watercolor or ink wash.

It's a good idea to use one of these—there's nothing worse than having your nicely inked drawing ruined by an accidental drop of water!

BRUSHES

Some artists like to use a fine brush for inking linework. This takes a bit more practice and patience to master, but the results can be very satisfying. If you want to try your hand at brushwork, you will definitely need to get some good-quality sable brushes.

ERASER

There are three main types of erasers: rubber, plastic, and putty. Try all three to see which kind you prefer.

PANTONE MARKERS

These are very versatile pens and with practice can give pleasing results.

INKS

With the rise of computers and digital illustration, materials such as inks have become a bit obscure, so you may have to look harder for these, but most good arts and crafts stores should stock them.

WATERCOLORS AND GOUACHE

Most art stores will stock a wide range of these products, from professional to student quality.

CIRCLE TEMPLATE

This is very useful for drawing small circles.

FRENCH CURVES

These are available in a few shapes and sizes and are useful for drawing curves.

BUILDING DINOSAURS

Notice how a simple oval shape forms the body of these three dinosaurs (figs.1, 2, and 3). Even though they are all very differently shaped, an oval forms the body of each one perfectly.

Fig. 4 shows how a dinosaur can be constructed using all these basic shapes. Cylinders are used for its legs and arms, an oval shape forms its body, and a smaller egg shape is used for its head.

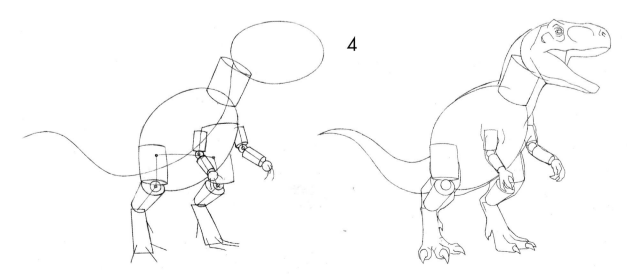

DRAWING CLAWS

Dinosaurs come in all shapes and sizes and so do their hands and feet. See the two columns below. On the left we have a Velociraptor's long thin digits, and on the right, a T. rex's stumpy claw. Although they look very different, both can be constructed using the same basic shapes.

VELOCIRAPTOR CLAW		T. REX CLAW

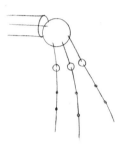

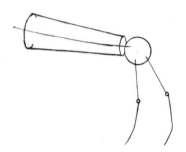

STEP 1

Draw a circle for the palm, a cylinder for the lower arm, and lines for the fingers. Use little circles to mark where the finger joints will go.

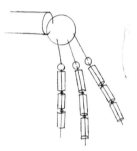

STEP 2

Use cylinder shapes to construct the thickness of the fingers. Velociraptor's are thin (see left) and T. rex's are fat (see right).

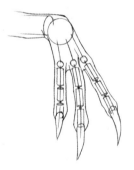

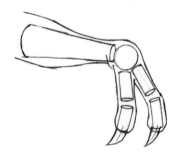

STEP 3

Now draw around the shapes to form the skin and add the claws.

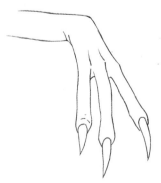

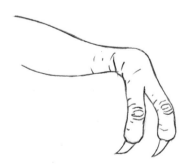

STEP 4

Finish off by erasing your construction shapes and adding some detail. Start to give a fleshy, textured appearance to the skin.

TYRANNOSAURUS REX

DINO FACT FILE

The superstar of the dinosaur world, *Tyrannosaurus rex* (meaning "tyrant lizard king") was a huge meat eater that lived about 65 million years ago. Its head was as big as a fridge, and it boasted about 50 teeth, each one longer than a human hand. Its massive skull was balanced by a long, heavy tail. T. rex had large, powerful back legs and relatively small arms with only two claws.

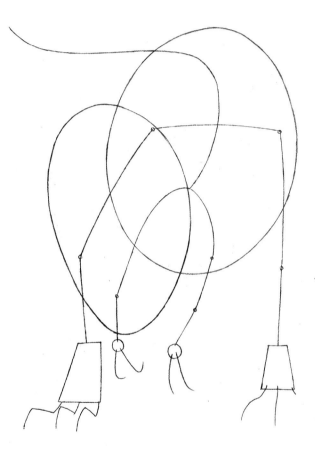

STEP 1
Start by drawing the basic stick figure.

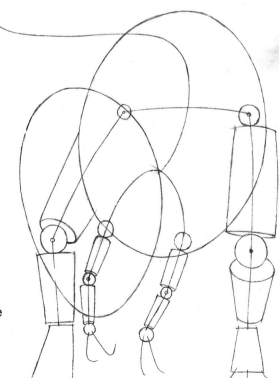

STEP 2
Now add the rest of the construction shapes.

STEP 3

Plot the T. rex's jaws
by drawing a line
across the middle of
the head, then add a
triangle underneath the
line. Add the claws
and tail, then remove
your stick-figure lines.

STEP 4

Now develop the T. rex's
distinctive head shape.
Draw in the face and
teeth. Go around the
construction shapes
to add the skin.

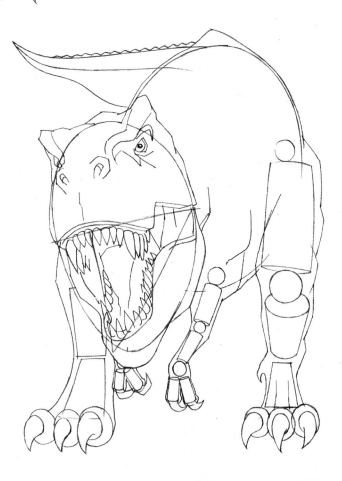

STEP 5

Carefully remove all your construction shapes and it's time to concentrate on the details. Add creases and scales to the skin, leaving the areas you want to shade blank.

STEP 6

Now it's time to add some shading and any fine details, as this is the final pencil stage.

STEP 7

Now ink over the pencil line. Bold shading will give your drawing perspective and a dramatic effect.

STEP 8

To color the T. rex, start with a sand-colored base. Then apply a midrange green on top. The base will make the green less vibrant and more like real reptile skin. Apply a midrange gray around the eyes and under the belly to add shade and depth. To color the mouth, use a light gray base then go over it with pink. Finish by adding a darker gray to add shape and depth.

VELOCIRAPTOR

DINO FACT FILE

Velociraptor (meaning "speedy raider") was a fast-running, two-legged dinosaur that preferred to hunt in a pack. This predator had about 80 very sharp, curved teeth in its long, flat snout. It had an S-shaped neck, three-fingered clawed hands, long thin legs, and four-toed clawed feet. One of these claws was particularly large and was a formidable weapon for sinking into its prey.

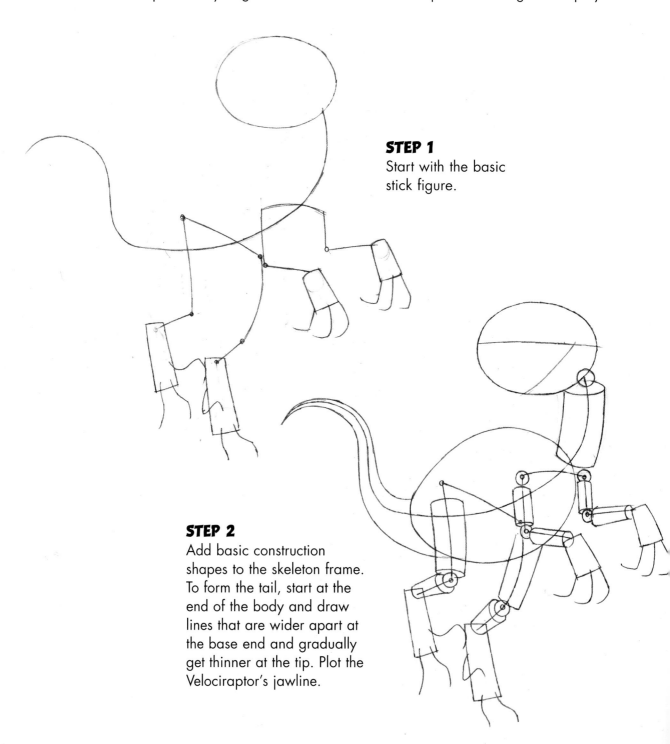

STEP 1

Start with the basic stick figure.

STEP 2

Add basic construction shapes to the skeleton frame. To form the tail, start at the end of the body and draw lines that are wider apart at the base end and gradually get thinner at the tip. Plot the Velociraptor's jawline.

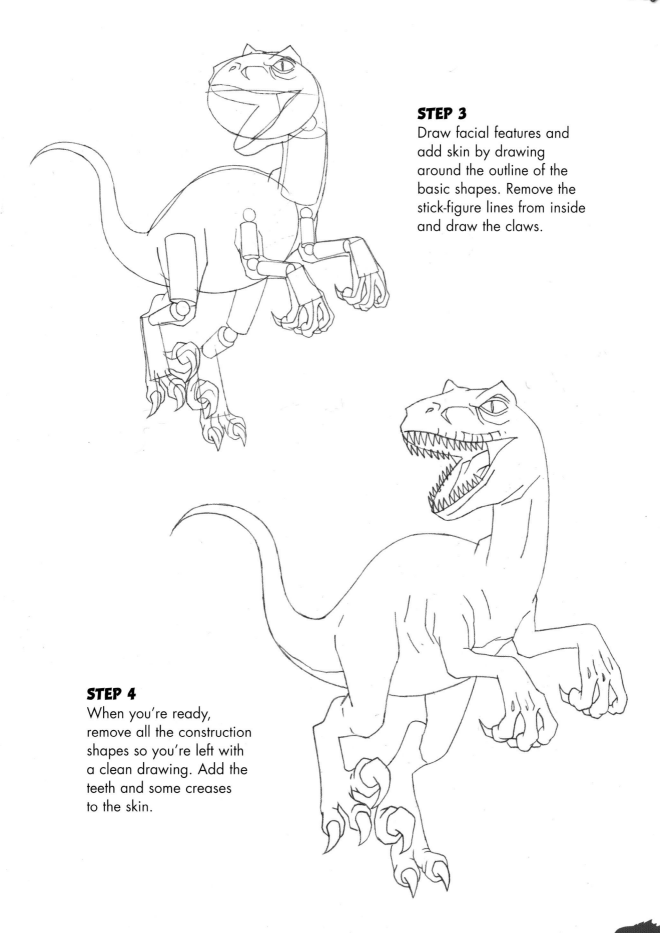

STEP 3
Draw facial features and add skin by drawing around the outline of the basic shapes. Remove the stick-figure lines from inside and draw the claws.

STEP 4
When you're ready, remove all the construction shapes so you're left with a clean drawing. Add the teeth and some creases to the skin.

STEP 5
Finish off the final pencil drawing by adding shading and any further detail.

DID YOU KNOW?
....
NEW RESEARCH SUGGESTS THAT VELOCIRAPTOR WAS ONLY ABOUT THE SIZE OF A LARGE DOG AND WAS COVERED IN FEATHERS.

STEP 6
Now ink over the pencil work.

STEP 7

Color the Velociraptor using a sand color for the skin base and warmer orange and red colors for along the back and head. Use a dark gray for the claws and finish off the skin using a midrange gray to create the stripes on the skin. Color the eye in bright yellow.

OVIRAPTOR

DINO FACT FILE

This birdlike predator's name means "egg thief" because the first fossil specimen was discovered on top of a pile of eggs. Scientists aren't sure if it preferred to eat meat, eggs, nuts, fish, insects, or a bit of everything. However, its sharp beak, claws, and the egg-breaking teeth on the roof of its mouth suggest it could take its pick. It grew to 6.6 feet (2 m) tall and was a fast runner.

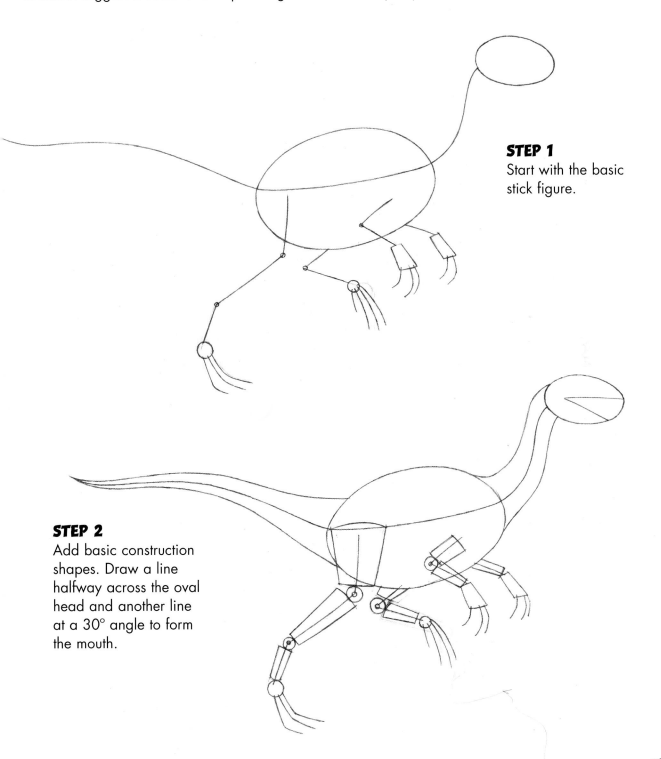

STEP 1
Start with the basic stick figure.

STEP 2
Add basic construction shapes. Draw a line halfway across the oval head and another line at a 30° angle to form the mouth.

STEP 3

Define Oviraptor's beaklike mouth and draw the facial features. Add skin and some feathers to the arms. Draw the claws and some creases in the skin. Remove all the basic stick lines.

STEP 4

Erase all of your interior construction shapes. Add more texture and depth to the skin. Draw feathers on its back, down the back of its neck, and add more to its arms. Notice how areas to be shaded in have been left blank.

STEP 5

Now complete the pencil
drawing by adding shading
and any additional detail
to the skin.

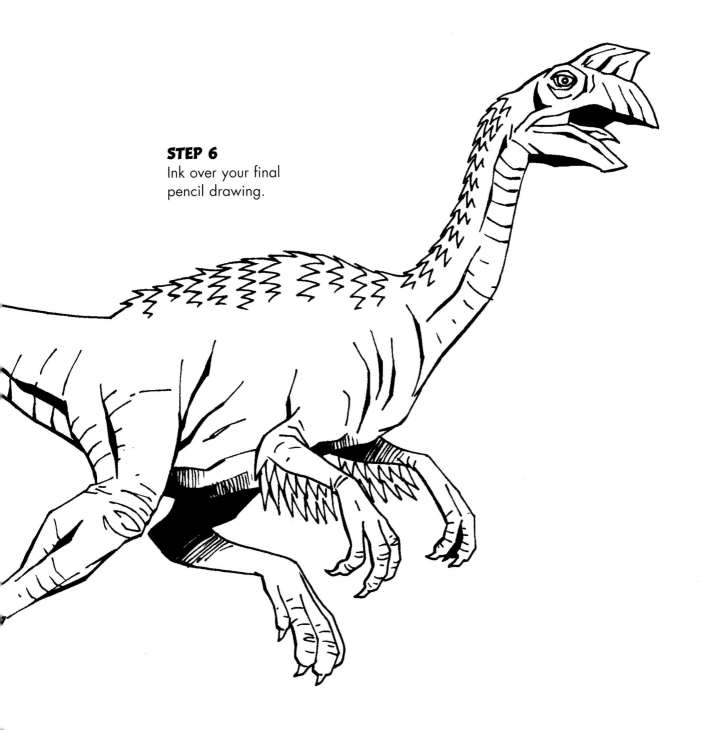

STEP 6
Ink over your final
pencil drawing.

STEP 7

Color the Oviraptor by starting with a sand-colored base. Add fuschia pink to the back of the neck and body, gradually fading down into the sand-colored belly. Now color the forearm feathers in bright green. Use a warm red for the crest on top of the head, and yellow for the beak and eye.

DID YOU KNOW?
OVIRAPTOR'S "EGG THIEF" NICKNAME MIGHT BE UNFAIR. AN OVIRAPTOR FOSSIL WAS FOUND ON A NEST OF ITS OWN EGGS. PERHAPS IT WASN'T STEALING!

CREATING A SCENE

LANDSCAPE FEATURING TYRANNOSAURUS REX

T. rex lived about 65 million years ago. This was the age when modern ecosystems developed. Many incredible creatures had evolved and this diversity was also found in the plants, flowers, and landscapes on Earth. T. rex roamed the plains and valleys of North America, where it would hunt plant eaters of all shapes and sizes.

STEP 1 Draw the horizon line just above the midpoint of the page. Sketch in some cliffs and a tree above the horizon line, and add leafy treelike plants to the foreground. Draw the stick figure for a T. rex. Add a lake in front of the cliff, just behind the dinosaur.

STEP 2 Construct the T. rex (see pages 9–13 for the step-by-step guide). Develop the leaves and cliff rock, and add three sets of dinosaur tracks in front of T. rex.

STEP 3 Work detail into the leaves and cliffside, and define the tracks. Add clouds, ferns, and a distant forest. Add teeth, claws, and facial features to the T. rex.

STEP 4 Complete the pencil drawing by adding shading to create areas of black and all your final details to the dinosaur and scenery.

STEP 5 Finally, color your prehistoric landscape. You could experiment with other colors to create different effects.

GLOSSARY

amazing (uh-MAYZ-ing) Wonderful.

cylinders (SIH-len-derz) Shapes with straight sides and circular ends of equal size.

facial (FAY-shul) Of the face.

gouache (GWAHSH) A mixture of nontransparent watercolor paint and gum.

jaws (JAHZ) Bones in the top and bottom of the mouth.

mechanical pencil (mih-KA-nih-kul PENT-sul) A pencil with replaceable lead that may be advanced as needed.

perspective (per-SPEK-tiv) In drawing, changing the relative size and appearance of objects to allow for the effects of distance.

sable brushes (SAY-bel BRUSH-ez) Artists' brushes made with the hairs of a sable, a small mammal from northern Asia.

stick figure (STIK FIH-gyur) A simple drawing of a creature with single lines for the head, neck, body, legs, and tail.

watercolor (WAH-ter-kuh-ler) Paint made by mixing pigments (substances that give something its color) with water.

INDEX

WEB SITES

Due to the changing nature of Internet links, PowerKids Press has developed an online list of Web sites related to the subject of this book. This site is updated regularly. Please use this link to access the list: www.powerkidslinks.com/ddino/trex/